# Patterns of Hope

## About this Anthology

On 9th April 2009 my sweetheart and beloved fiancé Bob Turner, sadly lost his battle with cancer. He was just 52 years old.

He was cared for with dignity at the Duchess of Kent House hospice in Reading, close to where he lived.

I live in North Yorkshire, and as a member of the Scarborough Poetry Workshop, I decided to draw upon the local wealth of poetic talent to help this hospice and potentially all other UK hospices, as well as those people who are facing difficult times.

I believe that poetry succeeds where mere words fall short of the mark. After losing Bob I found solace in poetry, and discovered that many more people have also found this so.

And this is how the idea for *Patterns of Hope* began. Through the gift that is poetry, I hope the poems found here can help many more to appreciate the gift that is life, no matter how long or short the journey.

*Sylvan Rose*

First published in Great Britain by Bob Turner Memorial Trust in association with Valley Press, 2009

ISBN 978-0-95-625194-7



Cover design by Gilly Collinson See: www.ioart.co.uk
Typeset in Minion by Mark Heslington, Scarborough, N Yorkshire
Printed and bound by McRay Press 01723 370967

# *Patterns of Hope*

**This copy sold by and in aid of:**

All of the proceeds from the sale of this book
will go towards the above.

Where this box is blank, the profit made from the sale of this copy will be used to produce more copies, which will then be given freely to more UK hospices.

On behalf of the people your purchase is helping,
thank you.

*Sylvan Rose*

Chair, Bob Turner Memorial Trust
www.BobTurnerMemorialTrust.org.uk

*In memory of Bob (I's alright) Turner,*
*with much love for one so greatly missed.*
*xxx*

# ACKNOWLEDGEMENTS

This anthology represents the efforts of many people, who have given their time and talents freely wherever possible.

So it is my pleasure to thank all of the poets for their wonderful contributions. I am eternally grateful to Gilly Collinson, for her excellent photographs and for producing the artwork for the cover. I thank Tracy Dunne for granting permission to use her beautiful painting '*Freedom*' to illustrate the poem *Shanaz*. Thanks also to Ian McMillan for his very kind contribution, and to Andy Boag for Ian's photograph.

I am indebted to Mark Heslington for typesetting the book without charge. Mike and Ray of McRay Press deserve every thanks for printing this book at a significant discount, making it possible to donate 75% of all copies, freely to UK hospices.

Thanks to Katherine Holmgren, who walked with me overnight from Scarborough to Whitby to help raise funds for the initial print-run, and Mark Witherington of the Grapevine Café in Whitby for feeding us at the end of the walk, and for raising further sponsorship.

For words of encouragement I thank my mum, Rita. And finally, I thank my beloved fiancé, Bob Turner, for still being my source of inspiration from his heavenly home. God bless you, sweetheart.

*Sylvan Rose*

# CONTENTS


Foreword by Ian McMillan 9
Tuesdays and Wednesdays *by Ian McMillan* 11
Daddy Long Legs *by Chris Woodland* 12
Rupayana *by Helen Burke* 13
Hands *by Anne Mullender* 14
Life's Boat *by Stuart Larner* 15
Voyage to a Distant Shore *by Sylvan Rose* 17
Pray *by Felix Hodcroft* 18
The Traveller *by Helen Burke* 19
The Sandman *by Katherine Holmgren* 20
Step of Faith *by David Agnew* 22
New Life *by Keith Butler* 24
A Helping Hand *by Sylvan Rose* 25
The Fourth Love *by Nigel Gerrans* 26
The Cloud Game *by Gilly Collinson* 28
Shades *by Sue Spivey* 30
Rumi's Field *by Chris Woodland* 31
Living in the Moment *by Deirdre McGarry* 33
My Granddaughter Saw Angels *by Norah Hanson* 34
Bridges *by Robert Anthony Johnson* 35
Dragonfly's Quest *by Sylvan Rose* 36
I Home *by Anne Mullender* 37
This One Leaf *by Stuart Larner* 39
The Walk Back Up *by Jamie McGarry* 40
The Concrete Path *by Norah Hanson* 42
Stretch Out Your Hand *by Keith Butler* 44
The Jesus Room *by Chris Woodland* 45
Colours in the Sky *by Gilly Collinson* 47

| | |
|---|---|
| Choral Evensong *by Nigel Gerrans* | 48 |
| The Meaning of Life *by Sylvan Rose* | 50 |
| Alex *by Helen Burke* | 52 |
| Shanaz *by Anne Mullender* | 55 |
| Decorations *by Stuart Larner* | 56 |
| Firefly *by Jamie McGarry* | 57 |
| The Wise Woman *by Katherine Holmgren* | 58 |
| Hurricane *by Sylvan Rose* | 60 |
| The Theft of Ordonnance *by Bob Jackman* | 62 |
| Thoughts on the Future *by Suzanne Marshall* | 63 |
| Life is but a Dream *by Robert (Bob) Turner* | 65 |
| Ammonite *by Gilly Collinson* | 66 |
| Exaltabo Te Deus *by Nigel Gerrans* | 67 |
| Trapeze *by Chris* Woodland | 68 |
| Love and Respect *by Sylvan Rose* | 69 |
| Poets' Brief Biographies | 71 |

Photograph by Andy Boag ©

# WORDS OF LIFE

Years ago I took part in an arts residency at St John's hospice in Doncaster; I went along to make poems, my friend Janet was there to make music, and my other friend Usha was there to make visual art with the people inside. We had a little meeting before the first visit and we were nervous; we thought somehow that the hospice would be a dark, gloomy place, with weeping relatives and desperately ill people and an institutional smell that covered another smell that none of us dared name. And, to my deep shame, I somehow thought in a strange way that terminal illness might be oddly catching, that I might come out of the place nearer to the end than I was when I went in.

How wrong we were, how wrong I was! Of course there was weeping and dreadful illness in the place, but there was also an overwhelmingly tangible sense of joy and happiness that was hard to put a finger on; it was about a celebration of life, about the living of it and the leaving of it, and of course I came out nearer the end than I was when I went in, but I came out fulfilled and more aware of the infinite power of the human spirit.

We worked with everyone in the hospice: the patients, the families, the nurses, the cleaners, the cooks, the man who'd come to deliver some parcels. And all the time we were making the poems and the songs and the art we were reminding each other and ourselves that in the end we're all creative beings, and that creativity can flourish everywhere.

So it's my delight to introduce these lovely, moving, skilful, exciting pieces of writing to you; there are moments of love, of pain, of delight, of pathos and of celebration. And each writer has taken time to communicate something to us, something that can help us through the dark times.

So, enjoy the book and, like I always say, have a go at writing your own poems because like those people in that hospice in Doncaster, we're all creative people.

*Ian McMillan*

# Tuesdays and Wednesdays

Ian McMillan, 2009

---

I imagined it would be a sad place,
The last room before death.
A place of tears and silence,
A slow dwindling to the last breath.
It isn't. It's a place of affirmation
That *now* is important, not the hereafter.
It taught me a lot: how to listen,
How to take each story as fresh and new,
How we can all teach each other a lesson,
How the telling of a life makes a life true.
And it confirmed what I'd suspected all along,
That everyone's artistic in a personal way,
Art's what makes us human and our song
Sings from the morning to the close of the day.

*Written after working at St John's Hospice, Doncaster.*

# Daddy Long Legs

Chris Woodland, 2004

---

Wrap him gently
In a handkerchief.
Carry him to the open window.
Watch him dance away
Into the autumn air.

However softly
The handkerchief closes
Round his delicate body
As he flutters helplessly
Within the folds,
How can he know
That in a moment
An unseen loving presence
Is about to release him
Into space and freedom?

# Rupayana

Helen Burke

*Rupayana came about through reading some works by Rabindrath Tagore, a marvellous Indian poet and mystic.*

On the banks of the Rupayana
I will read
what I will read
in the sand. You also in the sea
that flows there.

In the lighter part of night,
I see, green tassels, the beds of
five rivers and the gold lips
of collected lovers. They promise me
my youth again.

Draw tomorrow towards you.
Touch the soft fleece of it to the cheek.
Allow your dreams to kindle, burn.
Draw yourself love, light and laughter,
then

when your turn is come
to alight from the small boat
that battles against tall white waves,
you may read
what you may read
in the brilliance of the sand.

*Previously published in Dreamcatcher.*

# Hands

Anne Mullender, 1999

---

Grasp the hand of friendship
Hold it firm and tight

Shake the hand of welcome
Spread a little light

Touch the hand of love
Feel its warmth and might

Feed the hand of hunger
Fill the void tonight

Take the hand of healing
Ease the painful fight

Lift the hand of prayer
Let the soul take flight.

# Life's Boat

Stuart Larner

Once when my life did near submerge
They came to rescue me,
Called me to jump the crashing surge
To where I'd find safety.

At first I was afraid to make
That vault, so they did plead
'Your life comes from the leap you take!'
Thus I found truth in deed.

If problems since seem wide and deep
And can't be solved by Man,
I think back to that wondrous leap
For now I know I can.

*Previously published in the Gazette and Herald (North Yorkshire), 2008.*

Photograph by Sylvan Rose ©

# Voyage to a Distant Shore

Sylvan Rose, 2009

The bird that sings through metal bars
Gives of its love to all who hear.
Imprisoned, we respond and raise
A tiny smile, a poignant tear.
For love cannot be bound by walls,
Love transcends our mortal gaol.
It lifts the soul and lights the way –
It is the wind that fills our sail.
And we may cross those troubled seas
In search of those for whom we yearn,
And ask if those before us reached
That place from which none need return.

One day, perhaps, we will explore –
And find that distant, perfect shore,
Where loved ones live for ever more.

# Pray

Felix Hodcroft

---

Say that the summer had never ended,
say we could have wandered on a few miles
further east each day,
tracing the rim of that whispering sea,
pacing, racing the sun.

Say that our sun had never been smudged
and shrouded by English skies.

Say that those sparks flaring up from that fire
on that beach where we feasted on aubergine,
    bread, cheese and wine –

That those sparks were still vaulting
into pitch black heaven,
whose dazzling congregation
humming down upon us –

Say that those sparks, that pine wood, that
    summer
had never consumed themselves.

Say that your fingers still warm flesh in mine,
your lips still moist at my ear and saying this –

Say this.
Please say it.
Please.

# The Traveller

Helen Burke

Listen out for me,
who carves you out bright jewels
in the images of night
who sits at your window
to catch your eye as you awake.

There is no rock,
nor climbing hollow,
that is too far for us to travel
for tonight we're bound together
though they say I must away, but

Listen out for me, as there, –
there I go, – the traveller.
I am in your sudden softened footstep,
your ears' distant murmur,
even in your gaze as you
stand in wonder at the door –
keep a fire in your hearth for us
who travelled on at dawn.

# The Sandman

Katherine Holmgren, 1982

The sandman came
sprinkling his grains of gold
over tired eyelids
closed fast against the world,
closed fast against grim reality.

The sandman came
sprinkling his grains of gold,
'Cast off your bedclothes
and follow me'
he called.
'Follow me to the land of dreams;
Follow me to where the rainbow ends.'

The sandman came
sprinkling grains of gold.

I wanted to follow him
I wanted to go with him
over seas azure blue,
over fields of emerald green,
I wanted to follow him
and eagerly cast off the bedclothes.

But
the sandman went
taking with him his grains of gold,
for I was too slow,
too late.
It was no good,
I couldn't follow him this time.

The sandman went,
chased off by the shrill alarm
far away where I could not follow
hidden beyond the hope of the morning dawn.
Whilst I lay in my bed still processing
could I? would I? should I? DARE I?

I blinked open my eyes,
And dispersed the last few grains
and in my heart
I knew another time
when the sandman came
I would be ready.

Then I would happily follow.

# Step of Faith

David Agnew, 2009

---

Force of habit
creates patterns,
lays down tracks,
on which my mind
is used to walk.

Inertia
causes lethargy
which makes it
difficult to break
force of habit.

New pathways
are available
on which,
if I'm to grow,
I need to walk.

Courage, effort
are the attributes
which I most need
if I'm to walk
new pathways.

Trust, risk and share
the lady said
long time ago.
Her words resonate
with me again today.

Take deep breath,
put away dubious
comfort of walking
in old patterns.
Trust, risk and share.

**Photograph by Sylvan Rose ©**

# New Life

Keith Butler

---

Gently, I will lead you gently,
Along these paths.
To leave behind the old and spent
And find new life.

Softly, I will take you softly,
Within these arms
To hold you safe from pain and fear
And give you life.

Surely, I will love you surely,
For you are mine.
A precious child so rare, so dear.
And fill your life.

Truly, I will lift you truly
Above the plain.
To grow anew in heights above
And light your life.

# A Helping Hand

Sylvan Rose, 2004

*There can be no greater gift than a friendly hand to help us up when we are down. I dedicate this poem to my friend Dr Vernon Sykes, who has extended a helping hand to so many people.*

Sometimes as we make our way along life's dusty road,
We find a fellow traveller, and help him with his load.
We pause awhile and stand in awe, reflecting on the scene
That far below us fills the void, with shades of blue and green,
While onward, ever upward, the dusty road climbs high
And twists and turns, then vanishes amid the clouds and sky.
We know not where it leads us, but hope lives in our heart
And guides us on our journey; with love we play our part.
And when we stumble, there we find a helping hand appears
To lift us up and dust us down, and quell unspoken fears.
For life is more than what we see, far more than what we touch,
It lives in silent melodies, in dreams that mean so much,
It is the voice inside your head, the love within your heart,
The music of eternity, the purest work of art.
It needs no vows, nor charms or gifts, it is the air we breathe,
And all that should remain of us, when at last we leave.

# The Fourth Love

Nigel Gerrans, 1998

---

*Greek has four words for Love: one is for family affection; one for companionship and friendship; one for physical love; and the fourth (agapē) is the word used, particularly in the New Testament, for the self-giving, unconditional love that seeks only and always the good of the loved one.*

This is the love that holds me, still,
Despite the shifting sand;
Amid the anger, toil and fret
He shields me with his hand.

This is the love that never leaves
Despite my stubborn will;
That stays to calm, to ease, to heal,
The love that calls me still.

This is the love that crowns my life
When hurt and guilt assail,
When all I trust is broken down,
When all I try shall fail.

This is the love that knows my heart
When all I feel is shame;
Helps me to face my inner self
And calls me by my name.

It is a love that sets me free
When all around is fear;
A love that watches over me,
A love forever near.

Such a love believes in me
When all I know is doubt;
A love that always comes to me,
A love that seeks me out.

This is the love that holds me, still,
Despite the shifting sand;
Calls me to seek the higher way,
And guides me with his hand.

*Previously published in Selected Poems by Nigel Gerrans, River Seven Publishing, 2007.*

# The Cloud Game

Gilly Collinson

---

We're making shapes
From Summer clouds
(Oblivious to the crowds)

You find a cow
I, a crow
(Both real, we know)

We watch a mouse
Become a ray
(It flies away)

Such gentle games
Such precious hours
(Such cloudy showers)

You are my cumulo-
Nimbus friend
(Right to the end)

We hide ourselves
Amongst the stratus
(No world can part us)

Through cirrus wisps
We hide and seek
(Hush: do not speak)

Photograph by Sylvan Rose ©

# Shades

Sue Spivey

Fenced in,
We are restrained by barriers of silence;
Pain holds the gate closed:
Illusory safety,
a comforting denial
offering shelter and solace.

Beyond the gate,
beloved shades wait to share our lives.
Silent guides on an unseen path.

Take a small, gigantic step,
a deep crying breath.
In the dawn's light
we'll reclaim our courage.
We'll walk up to that gate
and push it open:
Taking a faltering step
back
to the future.

# Rumi's Field

Chris Woodland, 2005

---

*'Out beyond ideas of right-doing and wrong-doing there is a field. I'll meet you there.' Mevlana Rumi (1207–1273)*

At the gate
The patrolling angels
Take away
All your baggage
No matter how much
And wipe away
All your tears
No matter how many.

And then
They will open
The gate.

Go through
Into that field
Where there is always
The freshness of sunrise
And a new day breaking
Where the unjudgmental light
Is strong but gentle
Where you can feel
The power and the grace
Of your own energy and uniqueness
Where heart meets heart
And where you can
Celebrate and share
The truth and the poetry
Of who you really are.

Photograph by Sylvan Rose ©

# Living in the Moment

Deirdre McGarry

---

One magic morning an arrow of light
streamed through the woodland,
touched my awareness,
took me from my early morning kitchen
to become part of wings that soar and tunes that haunt,
rivers that gush and birds that burst.

I rode on a wild horse of fantasy,
danced to a gypsy beat,
climbed the high Andes,
heard the breathing pipes.
The green leaves of the trees
became the wet forest full of frogs and parrots.
The dew was mighty,
wet drops with rainbows passing through.

I tried to pin the butterfly moment
to trap it in a picture,
it subsided before my eyes.
Some days later it had faded,
I questioned what I had seen.

The truth is,
if I gaze in wonder,
gush and fly and sing,
let the moment touch my core,
then it never will be gone.

It is part of me.

# My Granddaughter Saw Angels

Norah Hanson

My granddaughter saw angels in flight
when the sky darkened to slate blue and
rooftop aerials gleamed in the sun's light.
'Look' she said, 'they've brought a rainbow.'
I saw them, bright silver winged arrows
swooping, darting, shining, as the arc
of the rainbow deepened in colour,
bands of red, gold, pink, green, purple
throbbing radiance in a holy sky.

My eyes became clear as washed windows,
reflecting polished verdure of tree and grass
freshly experienced reds of brick walls,
rain dropping diamonds through space
and all the while the winged messengers,
clothed in silver, dancing joy, flashing
against the dark translucence of the sky.

# Bridges

Robert Anthony Johnson, 2006

---

*Tarr Steps, Somerset*

You ask of me what these steps are
    for us to reach the same side.
But lost, in time now, are enigmas
    of how they once stood to greet,
To bless, to comfort, wrap in shawls
    wearisome travellers on their way.
Across this rugged simplicity,
    fifty-five metres wide,
Down through centuries, many thousands
    upon thousands of feet
Have trodden before us, to wear these stones
    to what we see today.

*The Millennium Footbridges*

Now we celebrate time and respect
    our own mortalities;
We build another one over The Thames,
    The Ouse and The Tyne.
We lay down plans to cross the most
    outrageous of divides
And forge social-economic ties
    between nationalities.
But the wood, the stone and the steel
    is all we will leave behind
And faith in these bridges to bind people
    beyond our own two lives.

*The complete version of 'Bridges' can be read online. See Poets' Brief Biographies for the website details.*

# Dragonfly's Quest

Sylvan Rose, 2009

---

Deep within the murky depths,
Mortality measured, calculated
By survival of the fittest,
Fastest, luckiest –
There lurks a creature
Camouflaged and overlooked.
For years it lurks, until
One day it answers a call
And begins to crawl
Upwards,
Towards the surface,
Into the light.

It cannot guess
Its vulnerability,
Nor know
Its outcome.
It simply answers a call,
A yearning deep within
To climb aloft
And shed its skin,

Then,
It soars upwards
Into the light.
Driven on
By need,
By nature,
And by faith.

# I Am Home

Anne Mullender, 2009

Train rattles on past harvested fields
where bales of hay wait to be carried away
labour fulfilled.
Tree branches weighed down,
waving like palm
as the wind gathers strength
under grey sky threatening rain.
At journey's end my friend greets me
welcomes me, arms opened wide,
smiling like warm rays of sunshine,
lighting up my heart…
I am home.

Photograph by Gilly Collinson ©

# This One Leaf

Stuart Larner, 2009

I found an autumn leaf you'd pressed
To be a marker in my book,
And as I turned each page I kept
The leaf close by me like your hand.

Now I've read through, I shelve the book
But will not shut your leaf away.
Instead I carry it with care
And tie it high back on its tree.

In winter's gales people ask 'Why
Doesn't that last flutterling fall?'
And I will answer 'Could it be
Someone waving who never left?'

# The Walk Back Up

Jamie McGarry, 2007

---

After town
We leave all of the lights
And noise and warmth and smells behind
We stagger up the hill
Blood freezing in our knees
Deafened by traffic

And we whine, we moan, we just want
    to get home
Have a cup of tea by the radiator
Listen to soothing tones
We cry 'I can't go on!'
'Till even that is too much effort
We become four silent figures, united in
    weariness
Beating a path in the pavement

And it's the knowing that the day is over
And the shuffling of our feet
That brings an air of understanding as we trudge
    back up the street
It is a calm, determined silence
For the last stretch is the toughest
Just the passing of the traffic
And our steady, heavy footsteps

When it's over, when we get there
We'll give a weary smile of thanks
We will fumble to unlock the doors,
And unload our heavy bags

But for now we all say nothing
Just stay silent, just stay climbing
We're four souls on automatic – and for a moment, we
    are heartless
But we push each other upwards,
Ever upwards, through the darkness

# The Concrete Path

Norah Hanson

*In Filey, summer of 2008.*

Three kites sail high above the Brig,
bright golden billows in the blue sky.
The sea is gentle, lapping over the feet
of grandparents, letting children leap
over incoming waves, rocking swimmers.

A solo cornet player in the Bandstand.
I hear again the tunes my father played
and seek refuge behind the hedge of
an enclosed garden where flower beds
blaze colour and silver lights the grass.

The wooden bench is named for a man
who loved this place; I breathe the air
he breathed and listen to your music.

A sparrow hops at my feet, pauses on
a tuft of infant grass sprouting in the
seam of the concrete path where
the dark grey meets the light grey.
And yesterday touches today.

Photograph by Sylvan Rose ©

# Stretch Out Your Hand

Keith Butler

Stretch out your hand in the darkness
You will find it being held.

When you're lonely and afraid,
And you cannot see your way.
Stretch out your hand in the darkness
You will find it being held.

When your burdens grow too heavy,
And you cannot carry on.
Stretch out your hand in the darkness
You will find it being held.

When pain or grief overwhelm you,
And you feel you cry alone.
Stretch out your hand in the darkness
You will find it being held.

Stretch out your hand in the darkness
You will find it being held.

# The Jesus Room

Chris Woodland, 1995

The Jesus room is not a chapel
Or a church or a shrine
Or anything like that.
It is not even sacred ground
In town or garden.
The Jesus room is inside the head,
Inside the heart, inside the body,
Inside the feelings, but no-one knows
Quite where the exact location is.
It is not really a room at all
And the Jesus discovered there
Does not come care of religious dogma
Or some archbishop or priest
Or politician or minister
Or anybody like that.
Indeed when you go into the Jesus room
You will find no-one there,
Only space ... emptiness ... energy.
You will, however, feel the vibrations
If you are very still and quiet.
And as you tune in to the power of the place
You will sense a presence, a mystery.
You will hear the poetry of the Jesus room.

*Previously published in The Young Oxford Book of Christmas Poems, O.U. P. 1995.*

Photograph by Gilly Collinson ©

# Colours in the Sky

Gilly Collinson

We watched a rainbow forming
It thrilled us with its hues
It found its shape from nowhere
Made from light and rain and blues.

Its definition clearer,
We picked out every shade
Through indigo to violet
We willed it not to fade.

Its colours grew so vivid,
We thought that it might stay,
But – fragile and ephemeral –
Our rainbow slipped away.

Now life is ever richer
For having seen that sight.
And will there be another?
Perhaps not – but there might.

# Choral Evensong

Nigel Gerrans, 1997

The old man watches you,
Watches you singing.
It is then his memories come,
And hints of somewhere beyond
Lift him from the darkness.
They will come from long before,
And will be always, after.
The old man watches you singing,
Your every movement,
Your concentrated energy
Dedicated
To the perfection of the music.

The old man listens,
Listens to you singing.
It is then the doors of perception
Open – your icons of sound
Lead him into worlds
Only a shadow's breath away,
And yet unknown
To those who pass, unaware.
They are there for him,
There for you; you meet
Where sound and colour,
Scent and touch
Elide, are one.
The old man listens,
Listens to you singing.

The old man sings with you,
Sings with you in his heart,
A heart you bring to life again,
A heart you lift
Into fields of fragrance
That are outside time
And beyond place,
Lift into the clearest air
Where winds flow, iridescent,
And angels call.
The old man sings with you
In his heart.

And somehow you can do this,
Somehow you can know,
Somehow you can tell him
Of a far greater beauty,
Where you share the mystery together,
The hurt and the joy,
The searching and the longing;
Where you share some of the answer
Which lies at the heart
Of the loving.
It is so,
It is ever so;
It has always been,
It will always be
So.

# The Meaning of Life

Sylvan Rose, 2003

---

*I find Ireland, the land of my forefathers, an inspirational place. I wrote this one fine summer's afternoon beside an ancient well up on the cliffs at Ardmore, County Waterford.*

In peaceful contemplation,
by O'Donnell's well I gaze
Across the cliffs, beyond the sea,
beyond the white-tipped waves
Into the distance, where I find
my inspiration's drawn
And blessed with creativity;
each moment I'm reborn.

To see afresh the blues and greens,
to hear the trembling grasses,
To drink in Nature's bounty,
as the summer slowly passes.
The sun beats down upon my face,
the warm wind's soft caress
Stirs my heart with joy and hope,
and love's sweet tenderness.
The scents of summer drift
upon the gentle tidal breeze,
And birdsong lifts the spirit,
while self-doubt simply flees.

It seems the reason we are here
    is borne of love so pure,
For life flows on and on,
    like endless waves upon the shore.
No nobler aim can we achieve:
    to leave no single trace
Except our love, that we might
    leave this world a better place.

**Photograph by Sylvan Rose ©**

# Alex

Helen Burke

Alex and I are regulars here.
We know the ropes.
Where to get a cup of tea if they've knocked off.
How to swing it for a late visitor.
Who will smile back, and who won't.

She's at one end of the building, I'm at the other.
It takes us an age to meet.
I can hear her cough before I see her.
She can glimpse my walking sticks –
the extra shadow they make on the wall.

We are too tired to speak when we meet.
So we lean on each other, and laugh.
Our curious profiles in the glass of the windows
like two circus clowns.
We share a coffee while we
get our breath back. Our breath is a constant
timebomb.
The corridor is the ringmaster. We forgive it.

None of this is satisfactory.

What we need, (Alex says) is a couple of miracles.
That's all.
Or one miracle, at least, that we could share.
Do you think there are such things as miracles?
Yes (I say) there must be another corridor,
one we haven't tried yet, one where breath lies thick
and lush like just laid carpet, smells like
new-mown grass. Let's go now, I say.

We set off down the long corridor.
Of course, (Alex says), I knew that all along.
A different corridor. Where miracles are spread out
for the taking, where we can both run and run and run
and nothing stops us. Neither breath, nor legs.

We link arms, set off in search of miracles.

© 'Freedom' by T.J.S. Dunne, 2009
See www.ArtTrendsByTracy.com

# Shanaz

Anne Mullender, 1998

---

Up and down the quiet beach
The golden mare flies along
Her platinum mane flowing
She shines in the morning sun.
Shanaz, stretches out from head to billowing tail,
Hot breath curling in the cool morning air
From flaring nostrils.

Her young rider allows her
To chase backwards and forwards
Alongside the water's edge.
Witnessing this flash of flaxen fringed gold
Is to seize the sheer exhilaration
Of absolute abandonment.
The pale wintry sun
Casts its cold light upon the morning sea
As determinedly the tide comes in.

Very soon horse and rider must return home
And leave behind this wide-open space.
Where, for a short while
Shanaz has spread her wings.

# Decorations

Stuart Larner

The season's passed; the trimmings come to floor
From where I'd fixed them at your well-judged
mark.
But your bright beauty won't go back to store
Along with lights that flashed once in the dark.
Your beauty needs no extra signs for me;
No festive letters shouting out 'Rejoice!'
In each ball's shining surface I still see
Your perfect face by any painter's choice.
Unlike full-fruited Nature, bought and pinned
Through its stem to wall at trophy height,
Your beauty's free – not bauble to be binned
Or boxed away in cupboards out of sight.
Now I will see in place of those things there
Not emptiness, but beauty all this year.

*Previously published in the Huddersfield Daily Examiner, 2007.*

# Firefly

Jamie McGarry, 2009

All too brief – but let's not, yet.
'This night's just getting started!'
Take my hand, and leap from this place,
swooping downwind past the fields.

We burn just once, but brightly –
these are the words of those rock 'n' roll tunes
(which are always the best for dancing to)

What once was dark has now turned bright,
so I do the things I normally do –
on a constant move to places new,
chased by the red light of my tail.

## The Wise Woman

Katherine Holmgren, 1988

*I dedicate this poem to my own Cree Indian ancestry.*

The wise woman sits,
her thoughts
like yarn all around her,

So come, sit by me
like children
and wind my thoughts
into balls of wisdom
to carry with you through life's journeys.

Carry my thoughts,
my words,
my deeds,
carry them within you,
unravel them as you wish,

Knit them into a blanket
to cover you
in your darkest hour,

Plant them like seeds
to grow into a tree
of knowledge
to aid you when you fear.

Pluck my words
like harp strings
to soothe the savage beast,

Eat my words and find succour
drink my words
and have no thirst,

For when all around
is your enemy,
only words of wisdom
will be
your friend.

# Hurricane

Sylvan Rose, 2009

---

At first a gentle breeze begins that
Lulls the treetops as she sings.
Then, more loudly stirs her call –
The boughs to sway, their crowns to fall,
Such joy to watch! A merry dance
Of leaves and tousled hair, enhanced
By vigour in the patterned skies,
Shapes that change, and tear-strewn eyes.

But strength is gained and words are lost –
Upon deaf ears is wisdom tossed
When brutal force meets weakened will,
Levelling the world, but still
In earnest does the pace proceed
To strip away the fruits of greed,
That we might see what truly matters
When far and wide, all else is scattered.

And still there's more, the fury flies
As focus zeroes on the prize
Oblivious to where each gust
Is blowing. Nothing matters, just
In knowing that the race is on –
It isn't over, isn't won …
Until we find how we are caught
Within the whirlwind. Bound and fraught
We gasp, and yet each laboured breath
Only seems to shepherd death.

But wait! What's this? Such peace and calm,
The storm's unassuming, healing balm –
Soft as a whispered name, begins to
Lull the enlightened soul that sings.

**Photograph by Sylvan Rose ©**

# The Theft of Ordonnance

Bob Jackman

---

Thoughts just out of reach.
Dreams in the busy daylight hours.
Glimpses of those but faintly remembered
On the distant fringes of this, I live my tangible life.

Should I awake and join this tangible world?
Or am I awake? Which world is mine?
I hear music. Mere wisps of melodies long forgotten,
Their sweetness fills me still and I lie content.

Age is lowering its grey mantle over me.
Beneath its dark folds I smile.

# Thoughts on the Future

Suzanne Marshall

When I was young
I could see the peaks clearly
The path seemed straight
Needing only my will and steadfast energy
To reach the glittering prize.

Now I look back
And am not even sure how the path became barred
Even what the prize was
Or was the prize after all worth it.

Yet the flame did not die
I glimpse it in my grandchild's laughing eyes
And smile content
He sees the peaks as once I did
And now no longer do
He sees the future bold and clear and full of light
And I see too
That nature's task is not to burn too bright
But simply to renew.

Photograph by Sylvan Rose ©

# Life is But a Dream

Robert (Bob) Turner, 2009

---

*Robert (Bob) Turner wrote many love poems to his sweetheart, Sylvan Rose, during the last six months of his life. He wasn't afraid to 'have a go', and this poem, collated from several others, proves what Ian McMillan says – we are indeed, all creative people.*

You entered my dreams that cold winter's night,
Your arm round my waist felt so very right.
As you lay here beside me, our bodies grew warm
Under the duvet in each other's arms.

No words are needed; my pains have all gone,
The touch of your love carries me on
Through the dark shadows, our love grows apace
As we greet each other and kiss and embrace.

Your soft silken skin, your head on my chest,
The smiles we share, so safe and so blessed.
The face that you show, I know you can't see
But a thousand words it speaks to me.

The taste of your lips is like a fine wine,
Softly my hand caresses your spine,
The other hand gently stroking your hair –
I know you are here, and you know I am there.

The pleasure is ours, as ever it was,
This night, tomorrow, forever – because
Love is a dream, and this dream has come true:
To lay here together, forever with you.

# Ammonite

Gilly Collinson

Spiral, cast up on the shore
True to mathematicians' law
Every chamber, every pore, a source of
fascination.

A creature of times long ago
Tectonic drift and lava flow
Formation of the world we know, deposit
and striation.

But aeons hence, are we here still?
And is survival luck or skill?
Might we endure through our freewill, or
predetermination?

**Photograph by Gilly Collinson ©**

# Exaltabo Te Deus

Nigel Gerrans, 1995

The experiments of Time are done,
And lessons learnt, a few;
Now I have come to hold at last
What perhaps I always knew.
It has taken a weary struggle
To climb the prison wall,
Not to reject who I really am,
But hear the inner call.
Much has been misused, much spoiled,
And many hurts remain,
But the hour has come to sift the gold,
To weigh the loss and gain;
Rejoice in the beauty I can know,
And praise through my delight,
Worship from the truth of me
Trusting it shall be right;
Bless with all my keenest sense,
Some of the wonder tell,
To leave a touch of loveliness,
And know all shall be well.

*Previously published in Selected Poems by Nigel Gerrans, River Seven Publishing, 2007.*

# Trapeze

Chris Woodland, 2008

---

*Just stretch out your arms and hands and trust, trust, trust.*
*Henri Nouwen.*

The clowns are leaving the ring
With squirts and somersaults.
In the wings your hands
Touch gently and your eyes
Meet in a whispered smile.
Loud and fast the band
Plays for your entrance.

The rope ladders fall.
Cat-like you climb lithely up
Higher and yet higher
To the crown of the tent.
You've no idea what it feels like
To be the focus of a thousand eyes.

Whatever you do now, don't look down.

The lights are dimming.
For a millisecond your whole life
Passes before you
As the drums roll.

Then grab the bar and fly, fly, fly
To those outstretched arms

And trust, trust, trust.

# Love and Respect

Sylvan Rose, 1997

*I have met many people in my time, and learned many things. Back in my student days a Russian man shared the following observation with me. There is little else to add. It is the only lesson we need to know.*

A wise man once asked me;
'Which would you select –
'The love of someone, or that person's respect?'

I pondered awhile, my mind was perplexed,
Which is the greater – love or respect?

'We all know the answer,' he said, 'I detect
'That love is the greatest form of respect.'

# Poets' Brief Biographies

**David Agnew** began writing poetry in 2005. He has had two books published – *Walking into Eternity* and *First I Dreamt the Journey*. His poetry has appeared in various publications and in public places – the walls of Leeds hospital waiting rooms and in the grounds of Nostell Priory. He writes primarily for himself and is delighted when others can identify with his words – his reflections on the Journey. See: www.walkingintoeternity.com

**Helen Burke** has been writing and performing poetry for about 35 years. Widely published in magazines and anthologies, winner of the Manchester Poetry Prize, Norwich Poetry Prize, Suffolk Poetry Prize, Sheffield Poetstars, Yorkshire Leslie Richardson Prize, Ilkley Literature Performance Prize and others. Currently being mentored by BBC to write for Radio, she did a solo show at Edinburgh Festival, and does some watercolour and printmaking. See: www.poetrypf.co.uk

**Keith Butler** was born in Bradford, and has since travelled the world. He spent time working as an electronics engineer, and started writing poetry in 1981 as a means of coming to terms with his wife's death after a very long illness. Through the grief he looked for hope and a future, and through his poetry he aims to show that beyond the darkness there is indeed light. Keith is now happily remarried and lives close to Scarborough.

**Gilly Collinson** grew up in York. She has composed poetry since early childhood, often accompanying her poems with illustrations. A graduate of Hornsey Art College, London, all her professional life has been dedicated to words and images. Writing for children as well as adults, she recited from the Fourth Plinth during Antony Gormley's *One and Other* project in 2009. Now living in Scarborough, her work encompasses words, digital media, photography, travel and beachcombing. See: www.ioart.co.uk

**Nigel Gerrans** was born in 1931, and educated in Epsom and at Emmanuel College, Cambridge. After working in a school for Cerebral Palsied children and in the Pharmaceutical Industry, he was ordained and served for many years as a full-time Chaplain in a busy District General Hospital. He has written poetry for over 50 years, and has recently had a collection, TENEBRAE, published by Valley Press. See: www.jamiemcgarry.com

**Norah Hanson** was born in Hull. She is a retired teacher and widow, with a large extended family. Her poems have been published in Iota, Dreamcatcher, Partners and other magazines. In the Bridport Poetry Competition she was long-listed in 2007 and short-listed 2009, and has had success in various other competitions. Email her at: nora.hanson@freenet.co.uk

**Felix Hodcroft,** Manchester-born and Oxford-bred, gained degrees in English Literature and Applied Social Sciences and worked as a probation officer in Birmingham, Hull and East Yorkshire. Studying, writing and performing poetry have been major factors in what limited success he has achieved in straddling life's tangled awfulness and glory and so he is proud to be a member and ex-Chair of Scarborough Poetry Workshop.

**Katherine Holmgren** moved from Whitby, North Yorkshire, in 1982 to Eire where the lyrical language shaped her poetry. She later tutored Creative Writing for Commonword and the WEA in Greater Manchester. Recently she did an MA in Expressive Therapies incorporating expressive arts with counselling and psychology in Massachusetts, USA. She has performed in the UK and the US, and volunteered for over five years at St Catherine's Hospice in Scarborough.

**Bob Jackman** was born in Glasgow in 1929 and from a tough beginning he rose to the position of Second Engineer Officer on British ships, and spent many years at sea. Writing became his pastime during these years, and he won a Channel Four TV competition, which helped him develop his talents further, and he now runs a Writers' Society which encourages poetry and prose.

**Robert Anthony Johnson** works with numbers by day, as an accountant, and moonlights with words as a poet. Born in Leeds, educated at the University of Northumbria and subsequently (as post graduate) at the University of Huddersfield, he is now settled in Scarborough. His work ranges from the immature verse of a teenager to the idiomatic poetry of a man commenting, with intelligent insight, on the world around him. Read more at: www.daylightpoetry.co.uk

**Stuart Larner** is a chartered clinical psychologist and writer. He was mental health expert for *XL for Men* magazine and has written self-help material and poems for various magazines, newspapers and local radio. He has also published numerous articles in scientific journals and at conferences. He has a wife and son, and lives in Yorkshire, UK. He is interested in cricket, and has short stories at: www.abcofcricket.com. See also: http://srlarner.awardspace.com/

**Suzanne Marshall** grew up in Scarborough but attended a Cumbrian boarding school where the dormitories were called after lake-land poets. She attributes her lifelong interest in verse to her Welsh origins and this early introduction to its delights. After some years abroad in Brussels and Saudi Arabia, she returned home. She feels her compulsive scribblings have been moulded and improved through membership of the Scarborough Poetry Workshop.

**Deirdre McGarry,** retired criminal lawyer, loved poetry as a teenager. She is greatly interested in the history, myths and legends of her home country, Ireland, and her poetry often reflects this. She is a founder member of award winning Irish poetry group, *Lucht Focail,* and has published an anthology *The Triple Spiral* with two other poets. She will shortly realise her own dream of returning to live in Ireland. Email: deirdre@lighthaven.fsnet.co.uk

**Jamie McGarry** (no relation of the above) was born in Norwich, in April 1988, and grew up in North Wales and Yorkshire. He currently lives in Scarborough, where he began studying for a degree in English Literature in 2008. His first collection, *What Do I Know Anyway?* was published in 2008, along with his first novel, *The Waiting Game.* His poems have appeared in The Dalesman, and various local papers. See: www.jamiemcgarry.com

**Anne Mullender**, born in Otley 1939, now lives in Bridlington. She had no intention of tackling the Poetry Module in a Creative Writing Course in 1995 but got hooked! Dubbed 'Larkinesque' her poetry gives her much pleasure, and when enjoyed by others is a bonus. Recently she was included in charity anthologies, *For the Kids* and *Not Dark Yet.* She was secretary for Bridlington Writers for nine years. You can email Anne at: annemullender246@btinternet.com

**Sylvan Rose** was born in Leeds, and now lives in Scarborough, North Yorkshire. She began writing poetry aged six, and has developed a very lyrical style that some have likened to Wendy Cope. She now uses her poetry to help raise funds for various charities, and as a member of the Scarborough Poetry Workshop, Sylvan performs her work at local venues throughout the year. Contact her at: www.BobTurnerMemorialTrust.org.uk

**Sue Spivey** was born in Hull but spent her early life in Zimbabwe and Zambia. She began writing seriously in her mid-thirties, and later graduated with a BA (Hons) in Creative Writing from Hull University. Sue's poetry is very visual and observational; small incidents or visual images acting as 'triggers' which she uses in her work. Sue is working on her first book of poetry entitled *Bubble Glass Moments* and will shortly complete her first novel *A month of Sundays*. She is a member of the Subtle Flame poetry group, which meets in Beverley. You can email Sue at: spivey16@spivey16.karoo.co.uk

**Chris Woodland,** educated at Scarborough and Cambridge, retired to Scarborough in 2004 after a varied and colourful teaching career in which creative approaches figured prominently. As a member of Scarborough Poetry Workshop, Chris has published an illustrated book of his poetry, *The Creative Spirit*. A framed poetry poster of *Daddy Long Legs* hangs in St Catherine's Hospice at Scarborough, where Chris himself has stayed as a patient.